DRAMATIS PERSONÆ

Austin   Mr. Harley.
Theodore   Mr. Bloomfield.
Fabian   Mr. Thompson.
Officers   Mr. Powell, Mr. Evatt.
The Count   Mr. Farren.
Adelaide   Mrs. Merry.
Jaqueline   Mrs. Platt.
Countess   Mrs. Pope.
Officers, Attendants, &c.

SCENE:—Narbonne Castle, and the Monastery of St. Nicholas, adjoining to the Castle.

THE COUNT OF NARBONNE

ACT THE FIRST

SCENE I

A Hall

Enter the **COUNT**, speaking to an Officer; **FABIAN** following.

COUNT
Not to be found! is this your faithful service?
How could she pass unseen? By hell, 'tis false!
Thou hast betray'd me.

OFFICER
Noble sir! my duty—

COUNT
Your fraud, your negligence—away, reply not.
Find her within this hour; else, by my life,
The gates of Narbonne shall be clos'd against thee;
Then make the world thy country.

[Exit **OFFICER**.

Fabian, stay!
Misfortunes fall so thick upon my head,

They will not give me time to think—to breathe.

FABIAN
Heaven knows, I wish your peace; but am to learn,
What grief more fresh than my young lord's decease,
A sorrow but of three days past, can move you.

COUNT
O bitter memory! gone, gone for ever!
The pillar of my house, my only son!

FABIAN
'Twas terrible indeed.

COUNT
Ay, was it not?
And then the manner of it! think on that!
Disease, that robb'd me of two infant sons,
Approaching slow, bade me prepare to lose them;
I saw my lilies drooping; and, accustom'd
To see them dying, bore to see them dead:
But, Oh my Edmund!—Thou remember'st, Fabian,
How blithe he went to seek the forest's sport!

FABIAN
'Would I could not remember!

COUNT
That cursed barb,
(My fatal gift) that dash'd him down the cliff,
Seem'd proud of his gay burden.—Breathless, mangled,
They bore him back to me. Fond man! I hoped
This day, this happy match with Isabel
Had made our line perpetual; and, this day,
The unfruitful grave receives him. Yes, 'tis fate!
That dreadful denunciation 'gainst my house,
No prudence can avert, nor prayers can soften.

FABIAN
Think not on that; some visionary's dream.
What house, what family could e'er know peace,
If such enthusiast's ravings were believ'd,
And phrensy deem'd an insight of the future?
But may I dare to ask, is it of moment
To stir your anger thus, that Isabel
Has left the castle?

COUNT

The Count of Narbonne by Robert Jephson

A TRAGEDY, IN FIVE ACTS

AS PERFORMED AT THE THEATRE ROYAL, COVENT GARDEN.

Robert Jephson was born in Ireland in 1736, the son of Archdeacon John Jephson.

His education was at Ryder's grammar school and then the Reverend Roger Ford's school before he was admitted to Trinity College, Dublin in 1751. He left without a degree.

Jephson now joined the British Army with a commission in the 73rd Regiment of Foot. Among his postings was one to the Caribbean. He left, for health reasons and retired with the rank of Captain.

An appointment was offered as master of the horse to the lord-lieutenant of Ireland. Whilst in this office he wrote and had published, in the Mercury newspaper, a collection of articles that defended the lord-lieutenant's administration. These were later published in book form as 'The Bachelor', or 'Speculations of Jeoffry Wagstaffe'.

Jepson held the office under twelve successive viceroys and gained a pension of £300, which was later doubled.

He entered the Irish House of Commons in 1773 and sat for St Johnstown (County Longford) until 1776. Between 1777 and 1783, he served as Member of Parliament for Old Leighlin and thereafter represented Granard from 1783 to 1790

In 1775 he added playwright, dramatist and poet to his military and political career strands. His plays gathered much interest. Among them his tragedy 'Braganza' was successfully performed at Drury Lane in 1775, 'Conspiracy' in 1796, 'The Law of Lombardy' in 1779, and 'The Count of Narbonne' (adapted from Horace Walpole's 'The Castle of Otranto') at Covent Garden in 1781.

In 1788 he published 'Extempore Ludicrous Miltonic Verses' and, in 1794, the heroic poem 'Roman Portraits', and 'The Confessions of Jacques Baptiste Couteau', a satire on the excesses of the French Revolution.

Robert Jephson died at Blackrock, near Dublin, on the 31st of May 1803.

Index of Contents

REMARKS

This tragedy was brought upon the stage in 1780; it was extremely admired, and exceedingly attractive.

Neither "The Winter's Tale", nor "Henry VIII" by Shakspeare, were at that time performed at either of the theatres; and the town had no immediate comparison to draw between the conjugal incidents in "The Count of Narbonne," and those which occur in these two very superior dramas.

The Cardinal Wolsey of Shakspeare, is, by Jephson, changed into a holy and virtuous priest; but his importance is, perhaps, somewhat diminished by a discovery, which was intended to heighten the interest of his character; but which is introduced in too sudden, and romantic a manner, to produce the desired consequence upon a well-judging auditor.

One of the greatest faults, by which a dramatist can disappoint and fret his auditor, is also to be met with in this play.—Infinite discourse is exchanged, numberless plans formed, and variety of passions agitated, concerning a person, who is never brought upon the stage—Such is the personal nonentity of Isabel, in this tragedy, and yet the fable could not proceed without her.—Alphonso, so much talked of, yet never seen, is an allowable absentee, having departed to another world; and yet, whether such invisible personages be described as alive, or dead, that play is the most interesting, which makes mention of no one character, but those which are introduced to the sight of the audience.

The lover of romances, whose happy memory, unclouded by more weighty recollections, has retained a wonderful story, by the late Lord Orford, called, "The Castle of Otranto," will here, it is said, find a resemblance of plot and incidents, the acknowledged effect of close imitation.

Lord Orford, (at that time Mr. Horace Walpole,) attended some rehearsals of this tragedy, upon the very account, that himself was the founder of the fabric.

The author was of no mean reputation in the literary world, for he had already produced several successful dramas. "The Count of Narbonne" proved to be his last, and his best composition.——Terror is here ably excited by descriptions of the preternatural—Horror, by the portraiture of guilt; and compassion, by the view of suffering innocence.—These are three passions, which, divided, might each constitute a tragedy; and all these powerful engines of the mind and heart, are here, most happily combined to produce that end,—and each forms a lesson of morality.

Of the deepest moment:
My best hope hangs on her; some future time,
I may instruct thee why.—These cares unhinge me:
Just now, a herald from her angry father
Left me this dire election—to resign
My titles, and this ample signory,
(Worthy a monarch's envy) or to meet him,
And try my right by arms. But pr'ythee tell,
(Nor let a fear to wound thy master's pride
Restrain thy licens'd speech) hast thou e'er heard
My father Raymond——(cast not down thine eye)
By any indirect or bloody means,
Procur'd that instrument, Alphonso's will,
That made him heir to Narbonne?

FABIAN
My best lord,
At all times would I fain withhold from you,
Intelligence unwelcome, but most now.
At seasons such as this, a friendly tongue
Should utter words like balm; but what you ask—

COUNT
I ask, to be inform'd of. Hast thou known me
From childhood, up to man, and canst thou fear
I am so weak of soul, like a thin reed,
To bend and stagger at such puny blast?
No; when the tempest rages round my head,
I give my branches wider to the air,
And strike my root more deeply.—To thy tale:
Away with palliatives and compliments;—
Speak plainly.

FABIAN
Plainly, then, my lord, I have heard
What, for the little breath, I have to draw,
I would not, to the black extent of rumour,
Give credit to.—But you command me speak—

COUNT
Thy pauses torture me.—Can I hear worse
Than this black scroll contains? this challenge here,
From Isabella's father, haughty Godfrey?
In broad, and unambiguous words, he tells me,
My father was a murderer, and forg'd
Alphonso's testament.

FABIAN

From Palestine,
That tale crept hither; where, foul slander says,
The good Alphonso, not, as we believe,
Died of a fever, but a venom'd draught,
Your father, his companion of the cross,
Did with his own hand mingle; his hand too,
Assisted by some cunning practisers,
Model'd that deed, which, barring Godfrey's right,
And other claims from kindred, nam'd Count Raymond
Lord of these fair possessions.

COUNT
Ha! I have it;
'Tis Godfrey's calumny; he has coin'd this lie;
And his late visit to the Holy Land,
No doubt, has furnish'd likelihood of proof,
To give his fiction colour.

FABIAN
Sure, 'tis so.

COUNT
He, too, has forg'd this idle prophecy,
(To shake me with false terrors) this prediction,
Which, but to think of, us'd to freeze my veins;
"That no descendant from my father's loins,
Should live to see a grandson; nor Heaven's wrath
Cease to afflict us, till Alphonso's heir
Succeeded to his just inheritance."
Hence superstition mines my tottering state,
Loosens my vassals' faith, and turns their tears,
Which else would fall for my calamities,
To gloomy pause, and gaping reverence:
While all my woes, to their perverted sense,
Seem but the marvellous accomplishment
Of revelation, out of nature's course.

FABIAN
Reason must so interpret. Good my lord,
What answer was return'd to Godfrey's challenge?

COUNT
Defiance.

FABIAN
Heaven defend you!

COUNT

Heaven defend me!
I hope it will, and this right arm to boot.
But, hark! I hear a noise.—Perhaps my people
Have found the fugitive.—Haste! bid them enter.

[Exit **FABIAN**.

She eyed me with abhorrence; at the sound
Of love—of marriage, fled indignant from me.
Yet must I win her: should she meet my wish,
Godfrey would prop the right he strives to shake,
Securing thus to his fair daughter's issue,
All that now hangs on the sword's doubtful point.

[Enter **OFFICER**.

Now, what tidings?
Where is the lady?

OFFICER
We have search'd in vain
The castle round; left not an aisle, or vault,
Unvisited.

COUNT
Damnation!

OFFICER
Near the cloister,
From whence, by the flat door's descent, a passage
Beneath the ground leads onward to the convent,
We heard the echo of a falling weight,
And sought it by the sound.

COUNT
Well, and what then?

OFFICER
The unsettled dust left us no room to doubt
The door had just been rais'd.

COUNT
She has escap'd,
And by confed'racy: to force that bar,
Without more aid, had baffled twice her strength.
Go on.

OFFICER

We enter'd; with resistance bold.
Theodore brought in by Fabian and Attendants.
This peasant push'd us backward from the spot.
My arm was rais'd to smite him, but respect
For something in his aspect, check'd the blow.
He, chiding, parleying by turns, gave time
For whosoever had descended there
(The lady doubtless) to elude our search:
The rest, himself will tell.

COUNT [To **THEODORE**]
Ha! what art thou?
Theodore. It seems, thy prisoner: disengage me first
From their rude grasp, and I may tell thee more.

COUNT
Unhand him. I should know thee; I have seen
Features like thine. Answer me, wert thou found
As these men say?

THEODORE
I was.

COUNT
And what thy purpose?

THEODORE
Chance brought me there.

COUNT
And did chance lead thee, too,
To aid a fugitive?

THEODORE
They saw not that.

COUNT
They saw it not! How! could her delicate hands,
Weak, soft, and yielding to the gentlest touch,
Sustain that pond'rous mass? No; those tough arms,
Thy force, assisted; else, thou young dissembler——

THEODORE
She had been seiz'd, and by compulsion brought
Where I stand now.

COUNT
Thou dost avow it then,

Boast it even to my face, audacious stripling!
Such insolence, and these coarse rustic weeds
Are contradictions. Answer me, who art thou?

THEODORE
Less than I should be; more than what I seem.

COUNT
Hence with this saucy ambiguity.
What is thy name, thy country? That mean habit,
Which should teach humbleness, speaks thy condition.

THEODORE
My name is Theodore, my country, France,
My habit little suited to my mind,
Less to my birth, yet fit for my condition.

COUNT
O, thou art then, some young adventurer,
Some roving knight, a hero in disguise,
Who, scorning forms of vulgar ceremony,
No leave obtain'd, waiting no invitation,
Enters our castles, wanders o'er our halls,
To succour dames distress'd, or pilfer gold.

THEODORE
There is a source of reverence for thee here,
Forbids me, though provok'd, retort thy taunts.

COUNT
If I endure this more, I shall grow vile
Even to my hinds—

THEODORE
Hold, let me stop thy wrath.
I see thy quivering lip, thy fiery eye,
Forerun a storm of passion. To prevent thee
From terms too harsh, perhaps, for thee to offer,
Or me to hear (poor as I seem) with honour,
I will cut short thy interrogatories,
And on this theme give thee the full extent
Of all I know, or thou canst wish to learn.

COUNT
Do it.

THEODORE
Without a view to thwart thy purpose.

(Be what it might), was I within thy walls.
In a dim passage of the castle-aisles,
Musing alone, I heard a hasty tread,
And breath drawn short, like one in fear of peril.
A lady enter'd, fair she seem'd, and young,
Guiding her timorous footsteps by a lamp;
"The lord, the tyrant of this place, (she cried)
For a detested purpose, follows me;
Aid me, good youth:" then pointing to the ground,
"That door," she added, "leads to sanctuary."
I seiz'd an iron hold, and, while I tugg'd
To heave the unwilling weight, I learn'd her title.

COUNT
The Lady Isabel?

THEODORE
The same. A gleam,
Shot from their torches, who pursued her track,
Prevented more; she hasten'd to the cave,
And vanish'd from my sight.

COUNT
And did no awe,
No fear of him, she call'd this castle's lord,
Its tyrant, chill thee?

THEODORE
Awe, nor fear, I know not,
And trust, shall never; for I know not guilt.

COUNT
Then thou, it seems, art master here, not I;
Thou canst control my projects, blast my schemes,
And turn to empty air my power in Narbonne.
Nay, should my daughter chuse to fly my castle,
Against my bidding, guards and bolts were vain:
This frize-clad champion, gallant Theodore,
Would lend his ready arm, and mock my caution.

THEODORE
Thy daughter! O, I were, indeed, too bless'd,
Could I but live to render her a service!

COUNT
My daughter, would, I hope, disdain thy service.

THEODORE

Wherefore am I to blame? What I have done,
Were it to do again, again I'd do it.
And may this arm drop palsied by my side,
When its cold sinews shrink to aid affliction!

COUNT
Indeed!

THEODORE
Indeed. Frown on.—Ask thy own heart,—
Did innocence and beauty bend before thee,
Hunted, and trembling, wouldst thou tamely pause,
Scanning pale counsel from deliberate fear,
And weigh each possibility of danger?
No; the instinctive nobleness of blood
Would start beyond the reach of such cold scruples,
And instant gratify its generous ardour.

COUNT [Aside]
I must know more of this. His phrase, his look,
His steady countenance, raise something here,
Bids me beware of him.—I have no time
To bandy idle words, with slaves like thee.
I doubt not thy intent was mischievous;
Booty perhaps, or blood. Till more inquiry
Clear, or condemn him, hold him in your guard.
Give none admittance—Take him from my sight.

THEODORE
Secure in her integrity, my soul
Casts back thy mean suspicions, and forgives thee.

[**THEODORE** is led out by **ATTENDANTS**.

COUNT
Away with him!—What means this heaviness?
My heart, that, like a well trimm'd, gallant bark,
Was wont to mount the waves, and dash them off
In ineffectual foam, now seems to crack,
And let in each assailing tide to sink me.
I must not yield to this dull lethargy.
Good Fabian, hie thee to Saint Nicholas';
Bid holy Austin straight repair to me.

[Exit **FABIAN**.

His sanctity, and reverend character,
His pious eloquence, made engines for me,

Might save a world of anguish to my soul,
And smooth my unwelcome purpose to Hortensia.
But how prevail with him?—Ambition?—No;
The world is dead in him, and gold is trash
To one, who neither needs, nor values it.
Interest and love shall wear the guise of conscience;
I must pretend nice scruples, which I feel not,
And make him mediate for me with the church.
Yet he reveres the countess; and, I fear,
Will spy more sin, in doubts that wound her quiet,
Than in my stifling them. But see, she comes,
With downcast eye, and sad, dejected mien.
I will not yet disclose it.

[Enter the **COUNTESS**.

Where's my child,
My all of comfort, now, my Adelaide?
COUNTESS
Dear as she is, I would not have her all;
For I should then be nothing. Time has been,
When, after three long days of absence from you,
You would have question'd me a thousand times,
And bid me tell each trifle of myself;
Then, satisfied at last, that all were well,
At last, unwilling, turn to meaner cares.

COUNT
This is the nature, still of womankind;
If fondness be their mood, we must cast off
All grave-complexion'd thought, and turn our souls
Quite from their tenour, to wild levity;
Vary with all their humours, take their hues,
As unsubstantial Iris from the sun:
Our bosoms are their passive instruments;
Vibrate their strain, or all our notes are discord.

COUNTESS
Oh, why this new unkindness? From thy lips
Never till now fell such ungentle words,
Nor ever less was I prepar'd to meet them.

COUNT
Never till now was I so urg'd, beset,
Hemm'd round with perils.

COUNTESS
Ay, but not by me.

COUNT

By thee, and all the world. But yesterday,
With uncontrollable and absolute sway
I rul'd this province, was the unquestion'd lord
Of this strong castle, and its wide domains,
Stretch'd beyond sight around me; and but now,
The axe, perhaps, is sharp'ning, may hew down
My perish'd trunk, and give the soil I sprung from,
To cherish my proud kinsman Godfrey's roots.

COUNTESS

Heaven guard thy life! His dreadful summons reach'd me.
This urg'd me hither. On my knees I beg,
(And I have mighty reasons for my prayer)
O do not meet him on this argument:
By gentler means strive to divert his claim;
Fly this detested place, this house of horror,
And leave its gloomy grandeur to your kinsman.

COUNT

Rise, fearful woman! What! renounce my birthright?
Go forth, like a poor, friendless, banish'd man,
To gnaw my heart in cold obscurity!
Thou weak adviser! Should I take thy counsel,
Thy tongue would first upbraid—thy spirit scorn me.

COUNTESS

No, on my soul!—Is Narbonne all the world?
My country is where thou art; place is little:
The sun will shine, the earth produce its fruits,
Cheerful, and plenteously, where'er we wander.
In humbler walks, bless'd with my child and thee.
I'd think it Eden in some lonely vale,
Nor heave one sigh for these proud battlements.

COUNT

Such flowery softness suits not matron lips.
But thou hast mighty reasons for thy prayer:
They should be mighty reasons, to persuade
Their rightful lord to leave his large possessions,
A soldier challeng'd, to decline the combat.

COUNTESS

And are not prodigies, then, mighty reasons?
The owl mistakes his season, in broad day
Screaming his hideous omens; spectres glide,
Gibbering and pointing as we pass along;

While the deep earth's unorganized caves
Send forth wild sounds, and clamours, terrible;
These towers shake round us, though the untroubled air
Stagnates to lethargy:—our children perish,
And new disasters blacken every hour.
Blood shed unrighteously, blood unappeas'd,
(Though we are guiltless,) cries, I fear, for vengeance.

COUNT
Blood shed unrighteously! have I shed blood?
No; nature's common frailties set aside,
I'll meet my audit boldly.

COUNTESS
Mighty Lord!
O! not on us, with justice too severe,
Visit the sin, not ours.

COUNT
What can this mean?
Something thou wouldst reveal, that's terrible.

COUNTESS
Too long, alas! it has weigh'd upon my heart;
A thousand times I have thought to tell thee all;
But my tongue falter'd, and refus'd to wound thee.

COUNT
Distract me not, but speak.

COUNTESS
I must. Your father
Was wise, brave, politic; but mad ambition,
(Heaven pardon him!) it prompts to desperate deeds.

COUNT
I scarce can breathe. Pr'ythee be quick, and ease me.

COUNTESS
Your absence on the Italian embassy
Left him, you know, alone to my fond care.
Long had some hidden grief, like a slow fire,
Wasted his vitals;—on the bed of death,
One object seem'd to harrow up his soul,
The picture of Alphonso in the chamber:
On that, his eye was set.—Methinks I see him,
His ashy hue, his grisled, bristling hair,
His palms spread wide. For, ever would he cry,

"That awful form—how terrible he frowns!
See, how he bares his livid, leprous breast,
And points the deadly chalice!"

COUNT
Ha! even so!

COUNTESS
Sometimes he'd seize my hands, and grasp them close,
And strain them to his hollow, burning eyes;
Then falter out, "I am, I am a villain!
Mild angel, pray for me;—stir not, my child;
It comes again;—oh, do not leave my side."
At last, quite spent with mortal agonies,
His soul went forth—and Heaven have mercy on him!

COUNT
Enough! Thy tale has almost iced my blood.
Let me not think. Hortensia, on thy duty,
Suffer no breath like this to pass thy lips:
I will not taint my noble father's honour,
By vile suspicions, suck'd from nature's dregs,
And the loose, ravings of distemper'd fancy.

COUNTESS
Yet, Oh, decline this challenge!

COUNT
That, hereafter.
Mean time, prepare my daughter to receive
A husband of my choice. Should Godfrey come,
(Strife might be so prevented) bid her try
Her beauty's power. Stand thou but neuter, Fate!
Courage, and art, shall arm me from mankind.

[Exeunt.

ACT THE SECOND

SCENE I

A Chamber

Enter **FABIAN** and **JAQUELINE**.

FABIAN

No, no, it cannot be. My lord's commands
Were absolute, that none should visit him.

JAQUELINE
What need he know it?

FABIAN
But perchance he should?
The study of my life has been his pleasure;
Nor will I risk his favour, to indulge
Such unavailing curiosity.

JAQUELINE
Call it not so; I have kind counsel for him;
Which, if he follow it, may serve to speed
The hour of his deliverance, and appease
The unjustly-anger'd count.

FABIAN
Pray be content;
I dare not do it. Have this castle's walls
Hous'd thee nine years, and, art thou yet to learn
The temper of the count? Serv'd and obey'd,
There lives not one more gracious, liberal;
Offend him, and his rage is terrible;
I'd rather play with serpents. But, fair Jaqueline,
Setting aside the comeliness and grace
Of this young rustic, which, I own, are rare,
And baits to catch all women, pr'ythee tell,
Why are you thus solicitous to see him?

JAQUELINE
In me, 'twere base to be indifferent:
He was my life's preserver, nay, preserv'd
A life more precious: yes, my dear young mistress!
But for his aid, the eternal sleep of death
Had clos'd the sweetest eyes that ever beam'd.
Aloof, and frighted, stood her coward train,
And saw a furious band of desperate slaves,
Inur'd to blood and rapine, bear her off.

FABIAN
What! when the gang of outlaw'd Thiery
Rush'd on her chariot, near the wood of Zart,
Was he the unknown youth, who succour'd her
All good betide him for it.

JAQUELINE

Yes, 'twas he.
From one tame wretch he snatch'd a half-drawn sword,
And dealt swift vengeance on the ruffian crew.
Two, at his feet stretch'd dead, the rest, amaz'd,
Fled, muttering curses, while he bore her back,
Unhurt, but by her fears.

FABIAN
He should be worshipp'd,
Have statues rais'd to him; for, by my life,
I think, there does not breathe another like her.
It makes me young, to see her lovely eyes:
Such charity! such sweet benevolence!
So fair, and yet so humble! prais'd for ever,
Nay, wonder'd at, for nature's rarest gifts,
Yet lowlier than the lowest.

JAQUELINE
Is it strange,
Fair Adelaide and I, thus bound to him,
Are anxious for his safety? What offence
(And sure, 'twas unintended) could provoke
The rigorous count thus to imprison him?

FABIAN
My lord was ever proud and choleric;
The youth, perhaps unus'd to menaces,
Brook'd them but ill, and darted frown for frown:
This stirr'd the count to fury. But fear nothing;
All will be well; I'll wait the meetest season,
And be his advocate.

JAQUELINE
Mean time, repair to him;
Bid him be patient; let him want no comfort,
Kind care can minister. My lady comes.
May I assure her of your favour to him?

FABIAN
Assure her, that the man, who sav'd her life,
Is dear to Fabian as his vital blood.

[Exit.

[Enter **ADELAIDE**.

ADELAIDE
I sent thee to his prison. Quickly tell me,

What says he, does he know my sorrow for him?
Does he confound me with the unfeeling crew,
Who act my father's bidding? Can his love
Pity my grief, and bear this wrong with patience?

JAQUELINE
I strove in vain to enter. Fabian holds him,
By the count's charge, in strictest custody;
And, fearful to awake his master's wrath,
Though much unwilling, bars me from his presence.

ADELAIDE
Unkind old man! I would myself entreat him,
But fear my earnest look, these starting tears,
Might to the experience of his prying age
Reveal a secret, which, in vain, I strive
To hide from my own breast.

JAQUELINE
Alas, dear lady,
Did not your tongue reveal it, your chang'd mien,
Once lighter than the airy wood-nymph's shade,
Now turn'd to pensive thought and melancholy,—
Involuntary sighs,—your cheek, unlike
Its wonted bloom, as is the red-vein'd rose,
To the dim sweetness of the violet—
These had too soon betray'd you. But take heed;
The colour of our fate too oft is ting'd,
Mournful, or bright, but from our first affections.

ADELAIDE
Foul disproportion draws down shame on love,
But where's the crime in fair equality?
Mean birth presumes a mind uncultivate,
Left to the coarseness of its native soil,
To grow like weeds, and die, like them, neglected;
But he was born my equal; lineag'd high,
And titled as our great ones.

JAQUELINE
How easy is our faith to what we wish!
His story may be feign'd.

ADELAIDE
I'll not mistrust him.
Since the bless'd hour, that brought him first to save me,
How often have I listen'd to the tale!
Gallant, generous youth!

Thy sport, misfortune, from his infant years!—
Wilt thou pursue him still?

JAQUELINE
Indeed, 'tis hard.

ADELAIDE
But, oh, the pang, that these ungrateful walls
Should be his prison! Here, if I were aught,
His presence should have made it festival;
These gates, untouch'd, had leap'd to give him entrance,
And songs of joy made glad the way before him.
Instead of this, think what has been his welcome!
Dragg'd by rude hands before a furious judge,
Insulted, menac'd, like the vilest slave,
And doom'd, unheard, to ignominious bondage.

JAQUELINE
Your father knew not of his service to you?

ADELAIDE
No, his indignant soul disdain'd to tell it.
Great spirits, conscious of their inborn worth,
Scorn by demand, to force the praise they merit;
They feel a flame beyond their brightest deeds,
And leave the weak to note them, and to wonder.

JAQUELINE
Suppress these strong emotions. The count's eye
Is quick to find offence. Should he suspect
This unpermitted passion, 'twould draw down
More speedy vengeance on the helpless youth,
Turning your fatal fondness to his ruin.

ADELAIDE
Indeed, I want thy counsel. Yet, oh, leave me!
Find, if my gold, my gems, can ransom him.
Had I the world, it should be his as freely.

JAQUELINE
Trust to my care. The countess comes to seek you;
Her eye is this way bent. Conceal this grief;
All may be lost, if you betray such weakness.

[Exit.

ADELAIDE
O love! thy sway makes me unnatural.

The tears, which should bedew the grave, yet green,
Of a dear brother, turning from their source,
Forget his death, and fall for Theodore.

[Enter the **COUNTESS**.

COUNTESS
Come near, my love! When thou art from my side,
Methinks I wander like some gloomy ghost,
Who, doom'd to tread alone a dreary round,
Remembers the lost things, that made life precious,
Yet sees no end of cheerless solitude.

ADELAIDE
We have known too much of sorrow; yet, 'twere wise
To turn our thoughts from what mischance has ravish'd,
And rest on what it leaves. My father's love—

COUNTESS
Was mine, but is no more. 'Tis past, 'tis gone.
That ray, at last, I hoped would never set,
My guide, my light, through, fortune's blackest shades:
It was my dear reserve, my secret treasure;
I stor'd it up, as misers hoard their gold,
Sure counterpoise for life's severest ills:
Vain was my hope; for love's soft sympathy,
He pays me back harsh words, unkind, reproof,
And looks that stab with coldness.

ADELAIDE
Oh, most cruel!
And, were he not my father, I could rail;
Call him unworthy of thy wondrous virtues;
Blind, and unthankful, for the greatest blessing
Heaven's ever-bounteous hand could shower upon him.

COUNTESS
No, Adelaide; we must subdue such thoughts:
Obedience is thy duty, patience mine.
Just now, with stern and peremptory briefness,
He bade me seek my daughter, and dispose her
To wed, by his direction.

ADELAIDE
The saints forbid!
To wed by his direction! Wed with whom?

COUNTESS

I know not whom. He counsels with himself.

ADELAIDE
I hope he cannot mean it.

COUNTESS
'Twas his order.

ADELAIDE
O madam! on my knees—

COUNTESS
What would my child?
Why are thy hands thus rais'd? Why stream thine eyes?
Why flutters thus thy bosom? Adelaide,
Speak to me! tell me, wherefore art thou thus?

ADELAIDE
Surprise and grief—I cannot, cannot speak.

COUNTESS
If 'tis a pain to speak, I would not urge thee.
But can my Adelaide fear aught from me?
Am I so harsh?

ADELAIDE
Oh no! the kindest, best!
But, would you save me from the stroke of death,
If you would not behold your daughter, stretch'd,
A poor pale corse, and breathless at your feet,
Oh, step between me and this cruel mandate!

COUNTESS
But this is strange!—I hear your father's step:
He must not see you thus: retire this moment.
I'll come to you anon.

ADELAIDE
Yet, ere I go,
O make the interest of my heart your own;
Nor, like a senseless, undiscerning thing,
Incapable of choice, nor worth the question,
Suffer this hasty transfer of your child:
Plead for me strongly, kneel, pray, weep for me;
And angels lend your tongue the power to move him!

[Exit.

COUNTESS
What can this mean, this ecstacy of passion!
Can such reluctance, such emotions, spring
From the mere nicety of maiden fear?
The source is in her heart; I dread to trace it,
Must then a parent's mild authority
Be turn'd a cruel engine, to inflict
Wounds on the gentle bosom of my child?
And am I doom'd to register each day
But by some new distraction?—Edmund! Edmund!
In apprehending worse even than thy loss,
My sense, confused, rests on no single grief;
For that were ease to this eternal pulse,
Which, throbbing here, says, blacker fates must follow;

[Enter **COUNT** and **AUSTIN**, meeting.

COUNT
Welcome, thrice welcome! By our holy mother,
My house seems hallow'd, when thou enter'st it.
Tranquillity and peace dwell ever round thee;
That robe of innocent white is thy soul's emblem,
Made visible in unstain'd purity.
Once more thy hand.

AUSTIN
My daily task has been,
So to subdue the frailties we inherit,
That my fair estimation might go forth,
Nothing for pride, but to an end more righteous:
For, not the solemn trappings of our state,
Tiaras, mitres, nor the pontiff's robe,
Can give such grave authority to priesthood,
As one good deed of grace and charity.

COUNT
We deem none worthier. But to thy errand!

AUSTIN
I come commission'd from fair Isabel.

COUNT
To me, or to the Countess?

AUSTIN
Thus, to both.
For your fair courtesy, and entertainment,
She rests your thankful debtor. You, dear lady,

And her sweet friend, the gentle Adelaide,
Have such a holy place in all her thoughts,
That 'twere irreverence to waste her sense
In wordy compliment.

COUNTESS
Alas! where is she?
Till now I scarce had power to think of her;
But 'tis the mournful privilege of grief,
To stand excus'd from kind observances,
Which else, neglected, might be deem'd offence.

AUSTIN
She dwells in sanctuary at Saint Nicholas':
Why she took refuge there—

COUNT
Retire, Hortensia.
I would have private conference with Austin,
No second ear must witness.

COUNTESS
May I not,
By this good man, solict her return?

COUNT
Another time; it suits not now.—Retire.

[Exit **COUNTESS**.

You come commission'd from fair Isabel?

AUSTIN
I come commission'd from a greater power,
The Judge of thee, and Isabel, and all.
The offer of your hand in marriage to her,
WIth your propos'd divorce from that good lady,
That honour'd, injur'd lady, you sent hence,
She has disclos'd to me.

COUNT
Which you approve not:
So speaks the frowning prelude of your brow.

AUSTIN
Approve not! Did I not protest against it,
With the bold fervour of enkindled zeal,
I were the pander of a love, like incest;

Betrayer of my trust, my function's shame,
And thy eternal soul's worst enemy.

COUNT
Yet let not zeal, good man, devour thy reason.
Hear first, and then determine. Well you know,
My hope of heirs has perish'd with my son;
Since now full seventeen years, the unfruitful curse
Has fallen upon Hortensia. Are these signs,
(Tremendous signs, that startle Nature's order!)
Graves casting up their sleepers, earth convuls'd,
Meteors that glare my children's timeless deaths,
Obscure to thee alone?—I have found the cause.
There is no crime our holy church abhors,
Not one high Heaven more strongly interdicts,
Than that commixture, by the marriage rite,
Of blood too near, as mine is to Hortensia.

AUSTIN
Too near of blood! oh, specious mockery!
Where have these doubts been buried twenty years?
Why wake they now? And am I closetted
To sanction them? Take back your hasty words,
That call'd me wise or virtuous; while you offer
Such shallow fictions to insult my sense,
And strive to win me to a villain's office.

COUNT
The virtue of our churchmen, like our wives,
Should be obedient meekness. Proud resistance,
Bandying high looks, a port erect and bold,
Are from the canon of your order, priest.
Learn this, for here will I be teacher, Austin;
Our temporal blood must not be stirr'd thus rudely:
A front that taunts, a scanning, scornful brow,
Are silent menaces, and blows unstruck.

AUSTIN
Not so, my lord; mine is no priestly pride:
When I put off the habit of the world,
I had lost all that made it dear to me,
And shook off, to my best, its heat and passions.
But can I hold in horror this ill deed,
And dress my brow in false approving smiles?
No: could I carry lightning in my eye,
Or roll a voice like thunder in your ears,
So should I suit my utterance to my thoughts,
And act as fits my sacred ministry.

COUNT

O father! did you know the conflict here;
How love and conscience are at war within me;
Most sure, you would not treat my grief thus harshly.
I call the saints to witness, were I master,
To wive the perfect model of my wish,
For virtue, and all female loveliness,
I would not rove to an ideal form,
But beg of Heaven another like Hortensia.—
Yet we must part.

AUSTIN

And think you to excuse
A meditated wrong to excellence,
By giving it acknowledgment and praise?
Rather pretend insensibility;
Feign that thou dost not see like other men;
So may abhorrence be exchang'd for wonder,
Or men from cursing fall to pity thee.

COUNT

You strive in vain; no power on earth can shake me.
I grant my present purpose seems severe,
Yet are there means to smooth severity,
Which you, and only you, can best apply.

AUSTIN

Oh no! the means hang there, there by your side:
Enwring your fingers in her flowing hair,
And with that weapon drink her heart's best blood;
So shall you kill her, but not cruelly,
Compar'd to this deliberate, lingering murder.

COUNT

Away with this perverseness! Get thee to her;
Tell her my heart is hers; here deep engrav'd
In characters indelible, shall rest
The sense of her perfections. Why I leave her,
Is not from cloy'd or fickle appetite
(For infinite is still her power to charm;)——
But Heaven will have it so.

AUSTIN

Oh, name not Heaven!
'Tis too profane abuse.

COUNT

Win her consent.
(I know thy sway is boundless o'er her will,)
Then join my hand to blooming Isabel.
Thus, will you do to all most worthy service;
The curse, averted thus, shall pass from Narbonne;
My house again may flourish; and proud Godfrey,
Who now disputes, will ratify my title,
Pleas'd with the rich succession to his heirs.

AUSTIN
Has passion drown'd all sense, all memory?
She was affianc'd to your son, young Edmund.

COUNT
She never lov'd my son. Our importunity
Won her consent, but not her heart, to Edmund.

AUSTIN
Did not that speak her soul pre-occupied?
Some undivulg'd and deep-felt preference?

COUNT
Ha! thou hast rous'd a thought: This Theodore!
(Dull that I was, not to perceive it sooner!)
He is her paramour! by Heaven, she loves him!
Her coldness to my son; her few tears for him;
Her flight; this peasant's aiding her; all, all,
Make it unquestionable;—but he dies.

AUSTIN
Astonishment! What does thy phrensy mean?

COUNT
I thank thee, priest! thou serv'st me 'gainst thy will.
That slave is in my power. Come, follow me.
Thou shalt behold the minion's heart torn out;
Then to his mistress bear the trembling present.

[Exeunt.

ACT THE THIRD

SCENE I

A Hall

Enter **ADELAIDE, JAQUELINE** following.

JAQUELINE
Where do you fly? Heavens! have you lost all sense?

ADELAIDE
Oh, 'would I had! for then I should not feel;
But I have sense enough to know I am wretched,
To see the full extent of misery,
Yet not enough to teach me how to bear it.

JAQUELINE
I did not think your gentleness of nature
Could rise to such extremes.

ADELAIDE
Am I not tame?
What are these tears, this wild, dishevel'd hair?
Are these fit signs for such despair as mine?
Women will weep for trifles, bawbles, nothing.
For very frowardness will weep as I do:
A spirit rightly touch'd would pierce the air,
Call down invisible legions to his aid,
Kindle the elements.—But all is calm;
No thunder rolls, no warning voice is heard,
To tell my frantic father, this black deed
Will sink him down to infinite perdition.

JAQUELINE
Rest satisfied he cannot be so cruel
(Rash as he is) to shed the innocent blood
Of a defenceless, unoffending youth.

ADELAIDE
He cannot be so cruel? Earth and heaven!
Did I not see the dreadful preparations?
The slaves, who tremble at my father's nod,
Pale, and confounded, dress the fatal block?
But I will fly; fall prostrate at his feet;
If nature is not quite extinguish'd in him,
My prayers, my tears, my anguish, sure will move him.

JAQUELINE
Move him indeed! but to redoubled fury:
He dooms him dead, for loving Isabel;
Think, will it quench the fever of his rage,
To find he durst aspire to charm his daughter.

ADELAIDE
Did I hear right? for loving Isabel?
I knew not that before. Does he then love her?

JAQUELINE
Nothing I heard distinctly; wild confusion
Runs through the castle: every busy fool,
All ignorant alike, tells different tales.

ADELAIDE
Away, it cannot be. I know his truth.
Oh! I despise myself, that for a moment
(Pardon me, love!) could suffer mean suspicion
Usurp the seat of generous confidence.
Think all alike unjust, my Theodore,
When even thy Adelaide could join to wrong thee!

JAQUELINE
Yet be advis'd—

ADELAIDE
Oh, leave me to my grief.—
To whom shall I complain? He but preserv'd
My life a little space, to make me feel
The extremes of joy and sorrow. Ere we met,
My heart was calm as the unconscious babe.

[Enter **FABIAN**.

FABIAN
Madam, my lord comes this way, and commands
To clear these chambers; what he meditates,
'Tis fit indeed were private. My old age
Has liv'd too long, to see my master's shame.

ADELAIDE
His shame, eternal shame! Oh, more than cruel!
How shall I smother it! Fabian, what means he?
My father—him I speak of—this young stranger—

FABIAN
My heart is rent in pieces: deaf to reason,
He hears no counsel but from cruelty.
Good Austin intercedes, and weeps in vain.

JAQUELINE
There's comfort yet, if he is by his side.
Look up, dear lady! Ha! that dying paleness—

ADELAIDE
It is too much—Oh, Jaqueline!

JAQUELINE
She faints;
Her gentle spirits could endure no more.
Ha! paler still! Fabian, thy arm; support her.
She stirs not yet.

FABIAN
Soft, bear her gently in.

[**ADELAIDE** is carried out.

SCENE II

Enter **COUNT**, followed by **AUSTIN**.

AUSTIN
I do believe thee very barbarous;
Nay, fear thy reason touch'd; for such wild thoughts,
Such bloody purposes, could ne'er proceed
From any sober judgment;—yet thy heart
Will sure recoil at this.

COUNT
Why, think so still;
Think me both ruffian-like, and lunatic;
One proof at least I'll give of temperate reason,—
Not to be baited from my fix'd design
By a monk's ban, or whining intercession.

AUSTIN
Thou canst not mean to do it.

COUNT
Trust thine eyes.
Thybalt! bring forth the prisoner; bid my marshal
Prepare an axe. The ceremony's short;
One stroke, and all is past. Before he die,
He shall have leave to thank your godliness,
For speeding him so soon from this bad world.

AUSTIN
Where is the right, the law, by which you doom him?

COUNT

My will's the law.

AUSTIN

A venerable law!
The law by which the tiger tears the lamb,
And kites devour the dove. A lord of France,
Dress'd in a little delegated sway,
Strikes at his sovereign's face, while he profanes
His functions, trusted for the general good.

COUNT

I answer not to thee.

AUSTIN

Answer to Heaven.
When call'd to audit in that sacred court,
Will that supremacy accept thy plea,
"I did commit foul murder, for I might?"

COUNT

Soar not too high; talk of the things of earth.
I'll give thee ear. Has not thy penitent,
Young Isabel, disclos'd her passion to thee?

AUSTIN

Never.

COUNT

Just now, her coldness to my son,
You said, bespoke her heart preoccupied.
The frail and fair make you their oracles;
Pent in your close confessionals you sit,
Bending your reverend ears to amorous secrets.

AUSTIN

Scoffer, no more! stop thy licentious tongue;
Turn inward to thy bosom, and reflect—

COUNT

That is, be fool'd. Yet will I grant his life,
On one condition.

AUSTIN

Name it.

COUNT

Join my hand
To Isabel.

AUSTIN
Not for the world.

COUNT
He dies.

[**THEODORE** brought in.

Come near, thou wretch! When call'd before me first,
With most unwonted patience I endur'd
Thy bold avowal of the wrong thou didst me;
A wrong so great, that, but for foolish pity,
Thy life that instant should have made atonement;
But now, convicted of a greater crime,
Mercy is quench'd: therefore prepare to die.

THEODORE
I was a captive long 'mongst infidels,
Whom falsely I deem'd savage, since I find
Even Tunis and Algiers, those nests of ruffians,
Might teach civility to polish'd France,
If life depends but on a tyrant's frown.

COUNT
Out with thy holy trumpery, priest! delay not,
Or, if he trusts in Mahomet, and scorns thee,
Away with him this instant.

AUSTIN
Hold, I charge you!

THEODORE
The turban'd misbeliever makes some show
Of justice, in his deadly processes;
Nor drinks the sabre blood thus wantonly,
Where men are valued less than nobler beasts.—
Of what am I accused?

COUNT
Of insolence;
Of bold, presumptuous love, that dares aspire
To mix the vileness of thy sordid lees
With the rich current of a baron's blood.

AUSTIN

My heart is touch'd for him.—Much injur'd youth,
Suppress awhile this swelling indignation;
Plead for thy life.

THEODORE
I will not meanly plead;
Nor, were my neck bow'd to his bloody block,
If love's my crime, would I disown my love.

COUNT
Then, by my soul, thou diest!

THEODORE
And let me die:
With my last breath I'll bless her. My spirit, free
From earth's encumbering clogs, shall soar above thee.
Anxious, as once in life, I'll hover round her,
Teach her new courage to sustain this blow,
And guard her, tyrant! from thy cruelty.

COUNT
Ha! give me way!

AUSTIN
Why, this is madness, youth:
You but inflame the rage you should appease.

THEODORE
He thinks me vile. 'Tis true, indeed, I seem so:
But, though these humble weeds obscure my outside,
I have a soul, disdains his contumely;
A guiltless spirit, that provokes no wrong,
Nor from a monarch would endure it, offer'd:
Uninjur'd, lamb like; but a lion, rous'd.
Know, too injurious lord, here stands before thee,
The equal of thy birth.

COUNT
Away, base clod.—
Obey me, slaves.—What, all amaz'd with lies?

AUSTIN
Yet, hear him, Narbonne: that ingenuous face
Looks not a lie. Thou saidst thou wert a captive—
Turn not away; we are not all like him.

THEODORE
My story's brief. My mother, and myself,

(I then an infant) in my father's absence,
Were on our frontiers seiz'd by Saracens.

COUNT
A likely tale! a well-devis'd imposture!
Who will believe thee?

AUSTIN
Go on, say all.

THEODORE
To the fierce bashaw, Hamet,
That scourge and terror of the Christian coasts,
Were we made slaves at Tunis.

AUSTIN
Ha! at Tunis?
Seiz'd with thy mother? Lives she, gentle youth?

THEODORE
Ah, no, dear saint! fate ended soon her woes,
In pity, ended! On her dying couch,
She pray'd for blessings on me.

AUSTIN
Be thou blessed!
O fail not, nature, but support this conflict!
'Tis not delusion, sure. It must be he.—
But one thing more; did she not tell thee too,
Thy wretched father's name?

THEODORE
The lord of Clarinsal.
Why dost thou look so eagerly upon me?
If yet he lives, and thou know'st Clarinsal,
Tell him my tale.

AUSTIN
Mysterious Providence!

COUNT
What's this? the old man trembles and turns pale. [Aside.

THEODORE
He will not let his offspring's timeless ghost
Walk unappeas'd; but on this cruel head
Exact full vengeance for his slaughter'd son.

AUSTIN
O Giver of all good! Eternal Lord!
Am I so bless'd at last, to see my son?

THEODORE
Let me be deaf for ever, if my ears
Deceive me now! did he not say his son?

AUSTIN
I did, I did! let this, and this, convince thee.
I am that Clarinsal; I am thy father.

COUNT
Why works this foolish moisture to my eyes? [Aside.
Down, nature! what hast thou to do with vengeance?

THEODORE
Oh, sir! thus bending, let me clasp your knees;—
Now, in this precious moment, pay at once
The long, long debt of a lost son's affection.

COUNT [Aside]
Destruction seize them both! Must I behold
Their transports, ne'er, perhaps, again to know
A son's obedience, or a father's fondness!

AUSTIN
Dear boy! what miracle preserved thee thus,
To give thee back to France?

THEODORE
No miracle,
But common chance. A warlike bark of Spain
Bore down, and seiz'd our vessel, as we rov'd
Intent on spoil: (for many times, alas!
Was I compell'd to join their hated league,
And strike with infidels.) My country known,
The courteous captain sent me to the shore;
Where, vain were my fond hopes to find my father:
'Twas desolation all: a few poor swains
Told me, the rumour ran he had renounc'd
A hated world, and here in Languedoc,
Devoted his remains of life to Heaven.

AUSTIN
They told thee truth; and Heaven shall have my prayers,
My soul pour'd out in endless gratitude,
For this unhoped, immeasurable blessing.

COUNT

Thus far, fond man! I have listen'd to the tale;
And think it, as it is, a gross contrivance—
A trick, devis'd to cheat my credulous reason,
And thaw me to a woman's milkiness.

AUSTIN

And art thou so unskill'd in nature's language,
Still to mistrust us? Could our tongues deceive,
Credit, what ne'er was feign'd, the genuine heart:
Believe these pangs, these tears of joy and anguish.

COUNT

Or true, or false, to me it matters not.
I see thou hast an interest in his life,
And by that link I hold thee. Wouldst thou save him,
Thou know'st already what my soul is set on,
Teach thy proud heart compliance with my will:
If not—but now no more.—Hear all, and mark me—
Keep special guard, that none, but by my order,
Pass from the castle. By my hopes of heaven,
His head goes off, who dares to disobey me!
Farewell!—if he be dear to thee, remember.

[Exit **COUNT**

AUSTIN

If he be dear to me! my vital blood!
Image of her, my soul delighted in,
Again she lives in thee! Yes, 'twas that voice,
That kindred look, rais'd such strong instinct here,
And kindled all my bosom at thy danger.

THEODORE

But must we bear to be thus tamely coop'd
By such insulting, petty despotism?
I look to my unguarded side in vain;
Had I a sword—

AUSTIN

Think not of vengeance now;
A mightier arm than thine prepares it for him.
Pass but a little space, we shall behold him
The object of our pity, not our anger.
Yes, he must suffer; my rapt soul foresees it:
Empires shall sink; the pond'rous globe of earth
Crumble to dust; the sun and stars be quench'd;

But O, Eternal Father! of thy will,
To the last letter, all shall be accomplish'd.

THEODORE
So let it be! but, if his pride must fall,
Ye saints, who watch o'er loveliness and virtue,
Confound not with his crimes, her innocence!
Make him alone the victim; but with blessings
Bright, and distinguish'd, crown his beauteous daughter,
The charming Adelaide, my heart's first passion!

AUSTIN
Oh most disastrous love! My son, my son,
Thy words are poniards here. Alas! I thought
(So thought the tyrant, and for that he rag'd)
The vows exchang'd 'tween Isabel and thee,
Thwarted the issue of his wild designs.

THEODORE
I knew not Isabel, beyond a moment
Pass'd in surprise and haste.

AUSTIN
O, had malignant fortune toil'd to blast him,
Thus had she snar'd him in this fatal passion!—
And does young Adelaide return thy love?

THEODORE
Bless'd powers, she does! How can you frown, and hear it!
Her generous soul, first touch'd by gratitude,
Soon own'd a kinder, warmer sympathy.
Soft as the fanning of a turtle's plumes,
The sweet confession met my enraptur'd ears.

AUSTIN
What can I do?—Come near, my Theodore;
Dost thou believe my affection?

THEODORE
Can I doubt it?

AUSTIN
Think what my bosom suffers, when I tell thee,
It must not, cannot be.

THEODORE
My love for Adelaide!

AUSTIN
Deem it delicious poison; dash it from thee:
Thy bane is in the cup.

THEODORE
O bid me rather
Tear out my throbbing heart; I'd think it mercy,
To this unjust, this cruel interdiction.
That proud, unfeeling Narbonne, from his lips
Well might such words have fallen;—but thou, my father—

AUSTIN
And fond, as ever own'd that tender name.
Not I, my son, not I prevent this union,
To me 'tis bitterness to cross thy wish,
But nature, fate, and Heaven, all, all forbid it.
We must withdraw, where Heaven alone can hear us:
Then must thou stretch thy soul's best faculties;
Call every manly principle to steel thee;
And, to confirm thy name, secure thy honour,
Make one great sacrifice of love to justice.

[Exeunt.

ACT THE FOURTH

SCENE I

A Chamber

ADELAIDE discovered.

ADELAIDE
Woe treads on woe.—Thy life, my Theodore,
Thy threaten'd life, snatch'd from the impending stroke,
Just gave a moment's respite to my heart;
And now a mother's grief, with pangs more keen,
Wakes every throbbing sense, and quite o'erwhelms me.
Her soul wrapp'd up in his, to talk thus to her!
Divorce her, leave her, wed with Isabel,
And call on Heaven, to sanctify the outrage!
How could my father's bosom meditate
What savage tongues would falter even to speak?
But see, he comes—

[Enter **AUSTIN** and **JAQUELINE**.

O let me bend to thank you;
In this extreme distress, from you alone
(For my poor heart is vain) can she hope comfort.

AUSTIN
How heard she the ill tidings? I had hopes
His cooler reason would subdue the thought;
And Heaven, in pity to her gentle virtues,
Might spare her knowing, how he meant to wrong them.

JAQUELINE
The rumour of the castle reach'd her first;
But his own lips confirm'd the barbarous secret.
Sternly, but now, he enter'd her apartment,
And, stamping, frown'd her women from her presence!
After a little while they had pass'd together,
His visage flush'd with rage and mingled shame,
He burst into the chamber where we waited,
Bade us return, and give our lady aid;
Then, covering his face with both his hands,
Went forth like one half-craz'd.

ADELAIDE
Oh good, kind father!
There is a charm in holy eloquence
(If words can medicine a pang like this)
Perhaps may sooth her. Sighs, and trickling tears,
Are all my love can give. As I kneel by her,
She gazes on me, clasps me to her bosom;
Cries out, My child! my child! then, rising quick,
Severely lifts her streaming eyes to heaven;
Laughs wildly, and half sounds my father's name;
Till, quite o'erpower'd, she sinks from my embrace,
While, like the grasp of death, convulsions shake her.

AUSTIN
Remorseless man! this wound would reach her heart,
And when she falls, his last, best prop, falls with her,
And see, the beauteous mourner moves this way:
Time has but little injur'd that fair fabric;
But cruelty's hard stroke, more fell than time,
Works at the base, and shakes it to the centre.

[Enter the **COUNTESS**.

COUNTESS
Will then, these dreadful sounds ne'er leave my ears?

Our marriage was accurs'd; too long we have liv'd
"In bonds forbid; think me no more thy husband;
The avenging bolt, for that incestuous name,
Falls on my house, and spreads the ruin wide."
These were his words.

ADELAIDE
Oh, ponder them no more!
Lo! where the blessed minister of peace,
He, whose mild counsels wont to charm your care,
Is kindly come to cheer your drooping soul;
And see, the good man weeps.

COUNTESS
What! weep for me?

AUSTIN
Ay, tears of blood from my heart's inmost core,
And count them drops of water from my eyes,
Could they but wash out from your memory
The deep affliction, you now labour with.

COUNTESS
Then still there is some pity left in man:
I judg'd you all by him, and so I wrong'd you.
I would have told my story to the sea,
When it roar'd wildest; bid the lioness,
Robb'd of her young, look with compassion on me;
Rather than hoped in any form of man,
To find one drop of human gentleness.

AUSTIN
Most honour'd lady!—

COUNTESS
Pray you, come not near me.
I am contagion all! some wicked sin,
Prodigious, unrepented sin, has stain'd me.
Father, 'twould blast thee but to hear the crimes,
This woman, who was once the wife of Raymond,
This curs'd forsaken woman here, has acted.

AUSTIN
What slanderous tongue dare thus profane your virtue?
Madam, I know you well; and, by my order,
Each day, each hour, of your unspotted life,
Might give as fair a lesson to the world,
As churchmen's tongues can preach, or saints could practise.

COUNTESS

He charges me with all—Thou, poor Hortensia!
What guilt, prepost'rous guilt, is thine to answer!

ADELAIDE

In mercy, wound not thus your daughter's soul.

AUSTIN

A villain or a madman might say this.

COUNTESS

What shall I call him? He, who was my husband;
My child, thy father;—He'll disclaim thee too.
But let him cast off all the ties of nature,
Abandon us to grief and misery—
Still will I wander with thee o'er the world:
I will not wish my reason may forsake me,
Nor sweet oblivious dulness steep my sense,
While thy soft age may want a mother's care,
A mother's tenderness, to wake and guard thee.

ADELAIDE

And, if the love of your dear Adelaide,
Her reverence, duty, endless gratitude
For all your angel goodness, now can move you,
Oh, for my sake (lest quite you break my heart)
Wear but a little outside show of comfort;
A while pretend it, though you feel it not,
And I will bless you for deceiving me.

COUNTESS

I know 'tis weakness—folly, to be mov'd thus;
And these, I hope, are my last tears for him.
Alas, I little knew, deluded wretch!
His riotous fancy glow'd with Isabel;
That not a thought of me possess'd his mind,
But coldness and aversion; how to shun me,
And turn me forth a friendless wanderer.

AUSTIN

Lady, for your peace,
Think, conscience is the deepest source of anguish:
A bosom, free like yours, has life's best sunshine;
'Tis the warm blaze in the poor herdsman's hut;
That, when the storm howls o'er his humble thatch,
Brightens his clay-built walls, and cheers his soul.

COUNTESS

O father, reason is for moderate sorrows;
For wounds which time has balm'd; but mine are fresh,
All bleeding fresh, and pain beyond my patience.
Ungrateful! cruel! how have I deserv'd it?
Thou tough, tough heart, break for my ease at once!

AUSTIN

I scarce, methinks, can weigh him with himself;
Vexations strange, have fallen on him of late!
And his distemper'd fancy drives him on
To rash designs, where disappointment mads him.

COUNTESS

Ah no! his wit is settled, and most subtle;
Pride and wild blood are his distemper, father.
But here I bid farewell to grief and fondness:
Let him go kneel, and sigh to Isabel:
And may he as obdurate find her heart,
As his has been to me.

AUSTIN

Why, that's well said;—
'Tis better thus, than with consuming sorrow
To feed on your own life. Give anger scope:
Time, then, at length, will blunt this killing sense;
And peace, he ne'er must know again, be yours.

COUNTESS

I was a woman, full of tenderness;
I am a woman, stung by injuries.
Narbonne was once my husband—my protector;
He was—what was he not?—He is my tyrant;
The unnatural tyrant of a heart, that lov'd him.
With cool, deliberate baseness, he forsakes me;
With scorn as steadfast shall my soul repay it.

AUSTIN

You know the imminent danger threatens him,
From Godfrey's fearful claim?

COUNTESS

Too well I know it;
A fearful claim indeed!

AUSTIN

To-morrow's sun
Will see him at these gates; but trust my faith,

No violence shall reach you. The rash count
(Lost to himself) by force detains me here.
Vain is his force:—our holy sanctuary,
Whate'er betides, shall give your virtue shelter;
And peace, and piety, alone, approach you.

COUNTESS
Oh, that the friendly bosom of the earth
Would close on me for ever!

AUSTIN
These ill thoughts
Must not be cherish'd. That all righteous Power,
Whose hand inflicts, knows to reward our patience:
Farewell! command me ever as your servant,
And take the poor man's all, my prayers and blessing.

[Exit **AUSTIN**.

ADELAIDE
Will you not strive to rest? Alas! 'tis long,
Since you have slept. I'll lead you to your couch;
And gently touch my lute, to wake some strain,
May aid your slumbers.

COUNTESS
My sweet comforter!
I feel not quite forlorn, when thou art near me.

ADELAIDE
Lean on my arm.

COUNTESS
No, I will in alone.
My sense is now unapt for harmony.
But go thou to Alphonso's holy shrine;
There, with thy innocent hands devoutly rais'd,
Implore his sainted spirit, to receive
Thy humble supplications; and to avert
From thy dear head, the still impending wrath,
For one black deed, that threatens all thy race.

[Exit **COUNTESS**.

ADELAIDE
For thee my prayers shall rise, not for myself,
And every kindred saint will bend to hear me.
But, O my fluttering breast!—'Tis Theodore!

How sad, and earnestly, he views that paper!
It turns him pale. Beshrew the envious paper!
Why should it steal the colour from that cheek,
Which danger ne'er could blanch? He sees me not.
I'll wait; and should sad thoughts disturb his quiet,
If love has power, with love's soft breath dispel them.

[Exit **ADELAIDE**.

[Enter **THEODORE**, with a Paper.

THEODORE
My importunity at last has conquer'd:
Weeping, my father gave, and bade me read it.
"'Tis there," he cried, "the mystery of thy birth;
There, view thy long divorce from Adelaide."
Why should I read it? Why with rav'nous haste
Gorge down my bane? The worst is yet conceal'd;
Then wherefore, eager for my own destruction?
Inquire a secret, which, when known, must sink me?
My eye starts back from it; my heart stands still;
And every pulse, and motion of my blood,
With prohibition, strong as sense can utter,
Cries out, "Beware!"—But does my sight deceive?
Is it not she? Up, up, you black contents:
A brighter object meets my ravish'd eyes.
Now let the present moment, love, be thine!
For ill, come when it may, must come untimely.

[Enter **ADELAIDE**.

ADELAIDE
Am I not here unwish'd for?

THEODORE
My best angel!
Were seas between us, thou art still where I am.
I bear thy precious image ever round me,
As pious men the relics they adore.
Scarce durst I hope to be so blest to see thee,
But could not wish a joy beyond thy presence.

ADELAIDE
O Theodore! what wondrous turns of fortune
Have given thee back to a dear parent's arms?
And spite of all the horrors which surround me,
And worse, each black eventful moment threatens,
My bosom glows with rapture at the thought

Thou wilt at last be bless'd.

THEODORE
But one way only
Can I be bless'd. On thee depends my fate.
Lord Raymond, harsh and haughty as he is,
And adverse to my father's rigid virtue,
When he shall hear our pure, unspotted vows,
Will yield thee to my wishes;—but, curs'd stars!
How shall I speak it?

ADELAIDE
What?

THEODORE
That holy man,
That Clarinsal, whom I am bound to honour,
Perversely bids me think of thee no more.

ADELAIDE
Alas! in what have I offended him?

THEODORE
Not so; he owns thy virtues, and admires them.
But with a solemn earnestness that kills me,
He urges some mysterious, dreadful cause,
Must sunder us for ever.

ADELAIDE
Oh, then fly me!
I am not worth his frown; begone this moment;
Leave me to weep my mournful destiny,
And find some fairer, happier maid, to bless thee.

THEODORE
Fairer than thee! Oh, heavens! the delicate hand
Of nature, in her daintiest mood, ne'er fashion'd
Beauty so rare. Love's roseate deity,
Fresh from his mother's kiss, breath'd o'er thy mould
That soft, ambrosial hue,—Fairer than thee!
'Twere blasphemy in any tongue but thine,
So to disparage thy unmatch'd perfections.

ADELAIDE
No, Theodore, I dare not hear thee longer;
Perhaps, indeed, there is some fatal cause.

THEODORE

There is not, cannot be. 'Tis but his pride,
Stung by resentment 'gainst thy furious father—

ADELAIDE
Ah no; he is too generous, just, and good,
To hate me for the offences of my father.
But find the cause. At good Alphonso's tomb
I go to offer up my orisons;
There bring me comfort, and dispel my fears;
Or teach me, (oh, hard thought!) to bear our parting.

[Exit **ADELAIDE**.

THEODORE
She's gone, and now, firm fortitude, support me!
For here I read my sentence; life or death.

[Takes out the Paper.

Thou art the grandson of the good Alphonso,
And Narbonne's rightful lord.—Ha! is it so?
Then has this boist'rous Raymond dar'd insult me,
Where I alone should rule:—yet not by that
Am I condemn'd to lose her. Thou damn'd scroll!
I fear thou hast worse poison for my eyes.
Long were the champions, bound for Palestine,
(Thy grandsire then their chief,) by adverse winds
Detain'd in Naples; where he saw, and lov'd,
And wedded secretly, Vicenza's daughter;
For, till the holy warfare should be clos'd,
They deem'd it wise to keep the rite conceal'd.
The issue of that marriage was thy mother;
But the same hour that gave her to the world,
For ever clos'd the fair one's eyes who bore her.
Foul treason next cut short thy grandsire's thread;
Poison'd he fell.—

[**THEODORE** pauses, and **AUSTIN**, who has been some time behind, advances.

AUSTIN
By Raymond's felon father,
Who, adding fraud to murder, forg'd a will,
Devising to himself and his descendants,
Thy rights, thy titles, thy inheritance.

THEODORE
Then I am lost—

AUSTIN

Now think, unkind young man,
Was it for naught I warn'd thee to take heed,
And smother in its birth this dangerous passion?
The Almighty arm, red for thy grandsire's murder,
Year after year has terribly been stretch'd
O'er all the land, but most this guilty race.

THEODORE

The murderer was guilty, not his race.

AUSTIN

Great crimes, like this, have lengthen'd punishments.
Why speak the fates by signs and prodigies?
Why one by one falls this devoted line,
Accomplishing the dreadful prophecy,
That none should live to enjoy the fruits of blood?
But wave this argument.—Thou wilt be call'd
To prove thy right,
By combat with the Count.

THEODORE

In arms I'll meet him;
To-morrow, now.—

AUSTIN

And, reeking with his blood,
Offer the hand, which shed it, to his daughter?

THEODORE

Ha!

AUSTIN

Does it shake thee?—Come, my Theodore,
Let not a gust of love-sick inclination
Root, like a sweeping whirlwind, from thy soul
All the fair growth of noble thoughts and virtue,
Thy mother planted in thy early youth;
Oh, rashly tread not down the promis'd harvest,
They toil'd to rear to the full height of honour!

THEODORE

Would I had liv'd obscure in penury,
Rather than thus!—Distraction!—Adelaide!

[Enter **ADELAIDE**.

ADELAIDE

Oh, whither shall I fly!

THEODORE
What means my love?
Why thus disturb'd?

ADELAIDE
The castle is beset;
The superstitious, fierce, inconstant people,
Madder than storms, with weapons caught in haste,
Menace my father's life; rage, and revile him;
Call him the heir of murderous usurpation;
And swear they'll own no rightful lord but Godfrey.

AUSTIN
Blind wretches! I will hence, and try my power
To allay the tumult. Follow me, my son!

[Exit **AUSTIN**.

ADELAIDE
Go not defenceless thus; think on thy safety,
See, yonder porch opes to the armoury;
There coats of mailed proof, falchions, and casques,
And all the glittering implements of war,
Stand terribly arrang'd.

THEODORE
Heavens! 'twas what I wish'd.
Yes, Adelaide, I go to fight for him:
Thy father, shall not fall ingloriously;
But, when he sees this arm strike at his foes,
Shall own, thy Theodore deserv'd his daughter.

[Exeunt.

ACT THE FIFTH

SCENE I

A Hall

Enter **COUNT, FABIAN, AUSTIN, ATTENDANTS** with **PRISONERS**.

COUNT
Hence to a dungeon with those mutinous slaves;

There let them prate of prophecies and visions;
And when coarse fare and stripes bring back their senses,
Perhaps I may relent, and turn them loose
To new offences, and fresh chastisement.

[Exeunt **OFFICERS**, &c.

FABIAN
You bleed, my lord!

COUNT
A scratch—death! to be bay'd
By mungrels! curs! They yelp'd, and show'd their fangs,
Growl'd too, as they would bite. But was't not poor,
Unlike the generous strain of Godfrey's lineage,
To stir the rabble up in nobles' quarrels,
And bribe my hinds and vassals to assault me.

AUSTIN
They were not stirr'd by Godfrey.

COUNT
Who then stirr'd them?
Thyself, perhaps. Was't thou? And yet I wrong thee;
Thou didst preach peace; and straight they crouch'd and shrunk,
More tam'd by the persuasion of thy tongue,
Than losing the hot drops my steel drew from them.

AUSTIN
I might, perhaps, have look'd for better thanks,
Than taunts to pay my service.—But no matter.—
My son, too, serv'd thee nobly; he bestrode thee,
And drove those peasants back, whose staves and clubs,
But for his aid, had shiver'd that stout frame:
But both, too well accustom'd to thy transports,
Nor ask, nor hope thy courtesy.

COUNT
Your pardon!
I knew my life was sav'd, but not by whom;
I wish'd it not, yet thank him. I was down,
Stunn'd in the inglorious broil; and nought remember,
More than the shame of such a paltry danger.
Where is he?

AUSTIN
Here.

[**THEODORE** advances from the Back of the Stage.

COUNT [Starting]
Ha! angels shelter me!

THEODORE
Why starts he thus?

COUNT
Are miracles renew'd?
Art thou not ris'n from the mould'ring grave?
And in the awful majesty of death,
'Gainst nature, and the course of mortal thought,
Assum'st the likeness of a living form,
To blast my soul with horror?

THEODORE
Does he rave?
Or means he thus to mock me?

COUNT
Answer me!
Speak, some of you, who have the power to speak;
Is it not he?

FABIAN
Who, good my lord?

COUNT
Alphonso.
His form, his arms, his air, his very frown.
Lord of these confines, speak—declare thy pleasure;

THEODORE
Dost thou not know me then?

COUNT
Ha! Theodore?
This sameness, not resemblance, is past faith.
All statues, pictures, or the likeness kept
By memory, of the good Alphonso living,
Are faint and shadowy traces, to this image!

FABIAN
Hear me, my lord, so shall the wonder cease.—
The very arms he wears, were once Alphonso's.
He found them in the stores, and brac'd them on,
To assist you in your danger.

COUNT
'Tis most strange.
I strive, but cannot conquer this amazement:
I try to take them off; yet still my eyes
Again are drawn, as if by magic on him.

AUSTIN [Aside to **THEODORE**]
Hear you, my son?

THEODORE
Yes, and it wakes within me,
Sensations new till now.

AUSTIN
To-morrow's light
Will show him wonders greater.—Sir, it pleas'd you,
(Wherefore you best can tell) to make us here
Your prisoners; but the alarm of your danger
Threw wide your gates, and freed us. We return'd
To give you safeguard.—May we now depart?

COUNT
Ay, to the confines of the farthest earth;
For here thy sight unhinges Raymond's soul.
Be hid, where air or light may never find thee;
And bury too that phantom.

[Exit **COUNT**, with his **ATTENDANTS**.

THEODORE
Insolence!
Too proud to thank our kindness! yet, what horror
Shook all his frame, when thus I stood before him!

AUSTIN
The statue of thy grandsire
(The very figure as thou stood'st before him,
Arm'd just as thou art), seem'd to move, and live;
That breathing marble, which the people's love
Rear'd near his tomb, within our convent's walls.
Anon I'll lead thee to it.

THEODORE
Let me hence,
To shake these trappings off.

AUSTIN

Wear them, and mark me.
Ere night, thy kinsman Godfrey, will be master
Of all thy story:—
He is brave, and just,
And will support thy claim. Should proof and reason
Fail with the usurper, thou must try thy sword
(And Heaven will strike for thee) in combat with him.
The conscious flash of this thy grandsire's mail,
Worse than the horrors of the fabled Gorgon,
That curdled blood to stone, will shrink his sinews,
And cast the wither'd boaster at thy feet.

THEODORE
Grant it ye powers! but not to shed his blood:
The father of my Adelaide, that name—

AUSTIN
Is dearer far than mine;—my words are air;
My counsels pass unmark'd. But come, my son!
To-night my cell must house thee. Let me show thee
The humble mansion of thy lonely father,
Proud once, and prosperous; where I have wept, and pray'd,
And, lost in cold oblivion of the world,
Twice nine long years; thy mother, and thyself,
And God, were all my thoughts.

THEODORE
Ay, to the convent!
For there my love, my Adelaide, expects me. [Aside.

[Exeunt.

SCENE II

Another Apartment in the Castle

Enter **COUNT** and **FABIAN**.

COUNT
By hell, this legend of Alphonso's death
Hourly gains ground.

FABIAN
They talk of naught besides;
And their craz'd notions are so full of wonder,
There's scarce a common passage of the times,

But straight their folly makes it ominous.

COUNT
Fame, that, like water, widens from its source,
Thus often swells, and spreads a shallow falsehood.
At first, a twilight tale of village terror,
The hair of boors and beldams bristled at it;
(Such bloodless fancies wake to nought but fear:)
Then, heard with grave derision by the wise,
And, from contempt, unsearch'd and unrefuted,
It pass'd upon the laziness of faith,
Like many a lie, gross, and impossible.

FABIAN
A lie believ'd, may in the end, my lord,
Prove fatal as a written gospel truth.
Therefore—

COUNT
Take heed; and ere the lightning strike,
Fly from the sulphurous clouds.—I am not dull;
For, bright as ruddy meteors through the sky,
The thought flames here, shall light me to my safety.
Fabian, away! Send hither to me straight,
Renchild and Thybalt.

[Exit **FABIAN**.

They are young and fearless.
Thy flight, ungrateful Isabel, compels me
To this rude course. I would have all with kindness;
Nor stain the snow-white flower of my true love
With spots of violence. But it must be so.
This lordly priest, this Clarinsal, or Austin,
Like a true churchman, by his calling tainted,
Prates conscience; and in craft abets Earl Godfrey,
That Isabel may wed his upstart son.
Let Rome dart all her lightnings at my head,
Till her grey pontiff singe in his own fires:
Spite of their rage, I'll force the sanctuary,
And bear her off this night, beyond their power;
My bride, if she consents; if not, my hostage.

[Enter **TWO OFFICERS**.

Come hither, sirs. Take twenty of your fellows;
Post ten at the great gate of Nicholas;
The rest, by two's, guard every avenue

Leads from the convent to the plain or castle.
Charge them (and as their lives shall answer it,)
That none but of my train pass out, or enter.

1ST OFFICER
We will, my lord, about it instantly.

COUNT
Temper your zeal, and know your orders first.
Take care they spill no blood:—no violence,
More than resisting who would force a passage:
The holy drones may buzz, but have no stings.
I mean to take a bawble from the church,
A reverend thief stole from me. Near the altar,
(That place commands the centre of the aisle)
Keep you your watch. If you espy a woman
(There can be only she), speed to me straight;
You'll find my station near Alphonso's porch.
Be swift as winds, and meet me presently.

[Exeunt severally.

SCENE III

The inside of a Convent, with Aisles and Gothic Arches

Part of an Altar appearing on one side; the Statue of Alphonso, in Armour, in the centre. Other Statues and Monuments also appearing. **ADELAIDE** veiled, rising from her knees before the Statue of Alphonso.

ADELAIDE
Alas! 'tis mockery to pray as I do.
Thoughts fit for heaven, should rise on seraphs' wings,
Unclogg'd with aught of earth; but mine hang here;
Beginning, ending, all in Theodore.
Why comes he not? 'Tis torture for the unbless'd,
To suffer such suspense as my heart aches with.
What can it be,—this secret, dreadful cause,
This shaft unseen, that's wing'd against our love?
Perhaps—I know not what.—At yonder shrine
Bending, I'll seal my irrevocable vow:
Hear, and record it, choirs of saints and angels!
If I am doom'd to sigh for him in vain,
No second flame shall ever enter here;
But, faithful to thy fond, thy first impression,
Turn thou, my breast, to every sense of joy,
Cold as the pale-ey'd marbles which surround me.

[ADELAIDE withdraws.

[Enter **AUSTIN** and **THEODORE**.

AUSTIN
Look round, my son! This consecrated place
Contains the untimely ashes of thy grandsire.
With all the impious mockery of grief,
Here were they laid by the dire hand which sped him.
There stands his statue; were a glass before thee,
So would it give thee back thy outward self.

THEODORE
And may the Power, which fashion'd thus my outside,
With all his nobler ornaments of virtue
Sustain my soul! till generous emulation
Raise me, by deeds, to equal his renown,
And—

AUSTIN
To avenge him. Not by treachery,
But, casting off all thoughts of idle love,
Of love ill-match'd, unhappy, ominous,—
To keep the memory of his wrongs; do justice
To his great name, and prove the blood you spring from.

THEODORE
Oh, were the bold possessor of my rights
A legion arm'd, the terrors of his sword
Resistless as the flash that strikes from heaven,
Undaunted would I meet him. His proud crest
Should feel the dint of no unpractis'd edge.
But, while my arm assails her father's life,
The unnatural wound returns to my own breast,
And conquest loses Adelaide for ever.

AUSTIN
The barbarous deed of Raymond's father lost her.

THEODORE
Pierce not my soul thus. Can you love your son,—
And coldly tell me,
Without one tear unmov'd thus, I must lose her?
But where, where is she?

[Looking out.

Heavenly innocence!
See, the dear saint kneels at the altar's foot;
See, her white hands with fervent clasps are rais'd;
Perhaps for me. Have you a heart, my father,
And bid me bear to lose her?—Hold me not—
I come, I fly, my life, my all! to join thee.

[Exit.

AUSTIN
Return, return, rash boy!—Pernicious chance!
One glance from her will quite destroy my work,
And leave me but my sorrow for my labour.

[Follows him.

[Enter **COUNT**.

COUNT
Am I turn'd coward, that my tottering knees
Knock as I tread the pavement?—'Tis the place;
The sombrous horror of these long-drawn aisles.
My footsteps are beat back by naught but echo,
Struck from the caverns of the vaulted dead;
Yet now it seem'd as if a host pursued me.
The breath, that makes my words, sounds thunder-like.
Sure 'twas a deep-fetch'd groan.—No;—hark, again!
Then 'tis the language of the tombs; and see!—

[Pointing to the Statue of Alphonso.

Like their great monarch, he stands rais'd above them.
Who's there?

[Enter **TWO OFFICERS**.

1ST OFFICER
My lord, where are you?

COUNT
Here—speak man!
Why do you shake thus? Death! your bloodless cheeks
Send fear into me. You, sir, what's the matter?

2ND OFFICER
We have found the lady.

COUNT

My good fellows, where?

1ST OFFICER
Here, from this spot, you may yourself behold her;
Her face is towards the altar.

COUNT [Looking out]
Blasts upon me!
Wither my eyes for ever!—Ay, 'tis she;
Austin with Theodore; he joins their hands:—
Destruction seize them! O dull, tardy fool!
My love, and my ambition, both defeated!
A marriage in my sight! Come forth! come forth!

[Draws a Dagger.

Arise, grim Vengeance, and wash out my shame!
Ill-fated girl! A bloody Hymen waits thee!

[Rushes out.

1ST OFFICER
His face is black with rage—his eyes flash fire;

I do not like this service.

2ND OFFICER
No, nor I.

1ST OFFICER
Heard you that shriek?—It thunders. By my soul,
I feel as if my blood were froze within me.
Speak to me. See he comes.

[**OFFICERS** retire.

[Enter **COUNT**, with a bloody Dagger.

COUNT
The deed is done.
Hark, the deep thunder rolls. I hail the sign;
It tells me, in loud greetings, I'm reveng'd.

[Enter **THEODORE**, with his Sword drawn.

THEODORE
Where, where's the assassin?

COUNT
Boy, the avenger's here.
Behold, this dagger smokes with her heart's blood!
That thou stand'st there to brave me, thank that mail,
Or, traitor, thou hadst felt me.—But 'tis done.

THEODORE
Oh, monstrous! monstrous!

COUNT
Triumph now o'er Narbonne;
Boast, how a stripling and a monk deceiv'd
The easy Count; but, if thou lov'st thy bride,
Take that, and use it nobly.

[Throws down the Dagger.

THEODORE
'Gainst thy heart,
Barbarian, would I use it: but look there;
There are ten thousand daggers.

AUSTIN [Without]
Ring out the alarm;
Fly all; bring aid, if possible, to save her.

[Enter **ADELAIDE**, wounded, and supported by **AUSTIN**. **THEODORE** advances to her, and assists in supporting and bringing her forward. Some of the Count's **ATTENDANTS** enter from the Castle, with lighted Torches.

COUNT
Ha! lightning shiver me!

ADELAIDE
My lord! my father!
Oh, bear me to his feet.

AUSTIN
Thou man of blood,
Past utterance lost; see what thy rage has done!

COUNT
Ruin! despair! my child, my Adelaide!
Art thou the innocent victim of my fury?

ADELAIDE
I am, indeed. I know not my offence;
Yet sure 'twas great, when my life answers it.

Will you forgive me now?

COUNT
Oh, misery!
Had I unnumber'd lives, I'd give them all,
To lengthen thine an hour. What phrensy seiz'd me!
That veil, the glimmering light, my rage, deceiv'd me.
Unnatural wound! detested parricide!—
Good youth, in pity strike this monster dead!

ADELAIDE
Listen not to his ravings.
[To **THEODORE**]
Alas, my Theodore!
I struggle for a little gasp of breath;
Draw it with pain; and sure, in this last moment,
You will observe me.—
Live, I charge you:
Forget me not, but love my memory.
If I was ever dear to thee, my father,
(Those tears declare I was,) will you not hear me,
And grant one wish to your expiring child?

COUNT
Speak, tell me quickly, thou dear, suffering angel!

ADELAIDE
Be gentle to my mother; her kind nature
Has suffer'd much; she will need all your care:
Forsake her not; and may the All-merciful
Look down with pity on this fatal error;
Bless you—and—oh—

[Dies.

COUNT
She dies in prayer for me;
Prays for me, while her life streams from my stroke.
What prayers can rise for such a wretch as I am?
Seize me, ye fiends! rouse all your stings and torments!
See, hell grows darker as I stalk before them.

THEODORE [After looking some time at **ADELAIDE'S** Body]
'Tis my black destiny has murder'd thee.
Stand off—

[They hold him.

I will not live.
This load of being is intolerable;
And, in a happier world, my soul shall join her.

[Rushes out.

AUSTIN
Observe, and keep him from all means of death.

[Enter **COUNTESS**, **FABIAN** and other **ATTENDANTS**.

COUNTESS
Whence were those cries? what meant that fearful bell?
Who shall withhold me? I will not return.
Is there a horror I am stranger to?

AUSTIN
There is; and so beyond all mortal patience,
I can but wish you stripp'd of sense and thought,
That it may pass without destroying you.

COUNTESS
What is it? speak—

AUSTIN [Looking towards the Body]
Turn not your eyes that way,
For there, alas—

COUNTESS
O Lord of earth and heaven!
Is it not she? my daughter, pale and bleeding!
She's cold, stark cold:—can you not speak to me?
Which of you have done this?

COUNT
'Twas ease till now;
Fall, fall, thick darkness, hide me from that face!

AUSTIN
Rise, madam, 'tis in vain.—Heaven comfort her!

COUNTESS
Shall I not strive to warm her in my breast?
She is my all; I have nothing left but her.
You cannot force me from her. Adelaide!
My child, my lovely child! thy mother calls thee.
She hears me not;—she's dead.—Oh, God! I know thee—
Tell me, while I have sense, for my brain burns;

Tell me—yet what avails it? I'll not curse—
There is a Power to punish.

COUNT
Look on me!
Thou hadst much cause to think my nature cruel;
I wrong'd thee sore, and this was my last deed.

COUNTESS
Was thine? thy deed? Oh, execrable monster!
Oh, greatly worthy of thy blood-stain'd sire!
A murderer he, and thou a parricide!
Why did thy barbarous hand refrain from me?
I was the hated bar to thy ambition;
A stab like this, had set thee free for ever;
Sav'd thee from shame, upbraiding, perjuries;—
But she—this innocent—what had she done?

COUNT
I thank thee. I was fool enough, or coward,
To think of life one moment, to atone
By deep repentance for the wrongs I did thee.
But hateful to myself, hated by thee;
By Heaven abandon'd, and the plague of earth,
This, this remains, and all are satisfied.

[Stabs himself.

Forgive me, if 'tis possible—but—oh—

[Dies.

COUNTESS [After looking some time distractedly]
Where am I? Ruin, and pale death surround me.
I was a wife; there gasping lies my husband!
A mother too; there breathless lies my child!
Look down, oh Heaven! look down with pity on me!—
I know this place;
I'll kneel once more. Hear me, great God of Nature!
For this one boon let me not beg in vain;
Oh, do not mock me with the hopes of death;
These pangs, these struggles, let them be my last;
Release thy poor, afflicted, suffering creature;
Take me from misery, too sharp to bear,
And join me to my child!

[Falls on the Body of **ADELAIDE**.

AUSTIN
Heaven comfort thee!—
Hard was your lot, thou lovely innocent;
But palms, eternal palms, above shall crown you.
For this rash man,—yet mercy's infinite,
[To the **COUNT**]
You stand amaz'd. Know, this disastrous scene,
Ending the fatal race, concludes your sorrows.
To-morrow meet me round this sacred shrine;
Then shall you hear at full a tale of wonder;
The rightful Lord of Narbonne shall be own'd;
And Heaven in all its ways be justified.

[Curtain falls.

www.ingramcontent.com/pod-product-compliance
Lightning Source LLC
Chambersburg PA
CBHW021942040426
42448CB00008B/1199